To my husband Joe,
whose support and encouragement
helped me complete this project.

To my daughter Michelle,
whose optimism and honesty
keep me on target.

To my parents
Don and Rose,
who taught me to always
be my best.

And to Stephanie Ward of TeleSet,
who helped me achieve my goal.

Publisher's Note: Additional copies of this manual are available for purchase. Other manuals in this series, posters, introductory packages and special prices for quantity purchases are also available. We are consistently updating and introducing new series. Please contact Bull'sEye Publishing at the address and phone listed below.

Second Printing, 2000, revised.
Third Printing, 2004

Customer Service 101: *Basic Lessons To Be Your Best*

Copyright © 1997, 2000 Renée Evenson

Library of Congress Catalog Card No.: 96-95312

ISBN 1-890181-00-5

PO Box 24024 • Saint Simons Island, GA 31522
(912) 638-0110 • Fax: (912) 634-7974
www.bullseyepublishing.com

PRINTED IN THE UNITED STATES OF AMERICA

Be Your Best

What does *Be Your Best* mean to you? These three simple words, put together, have a profound meaning. A meaning that can change your life. Totally and completely. Before you do anything, think these three words. Recite them to yourself. Make them your credo. And live by them. Whatever you do, give it your all, exceed your own expectations, surpass what you did yesterday, do everything with quality, think excellence. Always *Be Your Best*.

And if you do not quite know how to *Be Your Best* in your job, read this book. You will learn many valuable lessons that will help you to be your best.

Introduction

D o you get excited every time a customer walks into your business, each time you hear the phone ring? Do you eagerly drop what you are doing and enthusiastically greet your customers? Do you patiently answer all of their questions, and painstakingly make sure you do everything possible to make them happy? Do you swell with pride after helping customers, knowing you did your best for them?

Or do you find yourself resenting your customers? Do you think of them as an intrusion of your day? Do you think they are a nuisance when they expect you to drop everything and help them? Do they sometimes annoy you? And what about the ones who are not very nice to you?

All customers have similar qualities — they think only of themselves; they expect you to jump to meet their needs, to answer their questions, and do it all with a smile on your face! They do not care if they are keeping you from doing more important things. They want you to help them *now;* not when it is convenient for you. You are there to serve *them.* Do you ever find yourself thinking about how much easier your workday would be if they did not bother you?

Let's put that into perspective. Think about this. . . Say you get your wish. The customers stop coming or calling. What happens next? You probably are thrilled because now you have time to do your "job." But without those customers, business drops off. Your company is not making the money it used to. Your boss can no longer afford to pay you a salary because there are not enough customers bringing in enough cash to support you. So you get laid off.

What did you expect? It is not your company that pays your wages. It is those same customers you sometimes find so annoying. Do you still think they are a bother? Or do you now realize *they* are the reason you have a job?

This book is designed to help you improve your customer service skills; to be your best at work. Most customers you deal with are people just like you. They only want to be treated with respect and courtesy. This book provides invaluable tips on improving your customer skills. In the process, you will have more fun and get more satisfaction out of your job. And yes, there are customers who are truly annoying. Some people are just that way. There are tips to aid you in dealing with these types of people so they do not ruin your day.

Some of these tips will not be easy. But they can all be learned. Practice one at a time until it becomes natural for you. Then work on another. The best thing about learning them is they will help you in all aspects of your life.

Enjoy your work. That is the best advice anyone can give you.

Make It Exceptional

G iving good customer service is nothing more than observing the Golden Rule. Treat your customers the way you want to be treated as a customer. Giving exceptional customer service means going the extra mile by following the Golden Rule with enthusiasm and creativity.

Contents

Chapter 1

Basic Courtesies

R emember the basic courtesies we learned as children? Sometimes, as adults, we forget to use these simple, yet powerful words. As a customer service provider, they are most important. They show your customer you care.

1   Say please.

2   Say thank you.

3   Say you're welcome.

4   Say I'm sorry. I made a mistake.

5   Say excuse me.

6   Use *yes,* rather than *yeah.*

7   Say everything with a smile.

Chapter 2

Ethics

here is right and wrong. There is honesty and dishonesty. Do what is right. Do everything with honesty. That is ethics.

1   Always be honest. Your customers will know if you are not.

----

2   Never give a customer a reason to lose trust in you
or your company.

----

3   Integrity is the heart of success. One can never truly succeed
and be content without possessing this quality.

----

4   Do everything with integrity. *Everything.*

----

5   Do what you say you will, when you say you will.

----

6   Never knock your competition.
You will be the one who looks bad.

Chapter 3

Your Attitude

E very day you make a choice about your attitude. Before you make the choice for today, stop and think about your life. Think of all the things you have to be thankful for, the things your salary buys. Your home and furnishings, the car you drive, your clothes, food, vacations. The list is different for everyone, but without a salary you would not have the things you have.

You probably take all these things for granted. But when you think about who provides you with your salary, think about the customers who support your place of business. Without your customers, you would not have a job. When you go to work today, remember the people who really give you your paycheck. Show your customers how thankful you are that they chose your business.

1
    It is all in your presentation. ALL!

2
    Attitude is everything. Good *or* bad.
Your attitude is what your customers will remember
about your business.

3
    You may not get a second chance.

4
    Believe that *you* can make a difference.

5
    Leave your *"baggage"* at the door
when you come in to work.
Do not make your customers suffer
because you are having a bad day.

6
    Appreciate every day.

Be thankful you have a job.   7

If you find yourself becoming stressed,   8
take a break, get a drink of water, go for a short walk.
Just getting away from the situation for a few minutes
will help you put things in perspective.

Get enough rest. You will work better.   9

Make sure you do things for YOU every day.   10

Take care of exercising your mind and body.

Take time to have fun.

Take time to focus on your spiritual side.

You will be a better person,
have a better outlook, and be a better employee.

Chapter 4

Your Appearance

W hether you are more comfortable being sloppy or more comfortable being neat, it takes about the same amount of time to dress. And it does not take that much longer to keep your clothes clean and pressed. When you are at work, your appearance tells your customers who you are and what you think of yourself.

1   Customers will see you first, hear you second.

———————

2   Dress professionally. You will act more professionally.

———————

3   Make sure you are clean and groomed
when you are at work.

Clean means your
hair, body, hands, fingernails, and teeth are clean.

Groomed means you wear appropriate clothing
for the type of work you do, your clothes are pressed,
and your shoes are clean.

———————

4   Look in a full length mirror before you leave for work.

———————

5   You do not have to spend a fortune
on a business wardrobe to look professional.
It is not how much the clothes cost that is important;
it is how they look that is important.

Check yourself during the day.

6

Part of your appearance is your body language.
Hold your head high,
make eye contact with your customers,
maintain a natural smile,
and be relaxed and poised.

7

Chapter 5

Communicating Effectively

C ommunication is never one way. It always takes two to communicate. Be the one to initiate open, honest, and tactful communication with your customers and with your fellow employees. When you treat others in this manner, chances are they will treat you the same way.

People feel free to voice their thoughts and opinions when they feel they will be respected and supported. That is where trust begins. And trust is never freely given. It must always be earned. But when there is trust, there is the ability to establish and maintain a relationship.

1
Establish rapport with your customer.

———————

2
Erase the words "I can't" from your vocabulary.

———————

3
If you find you cannot do what your customer wants,
tell him what you CAN do.
Offer alternatives.

———————

4
Try very hard to avoid saying "no."

———————

5
Be conversational —
but do not be overly conversational.
Know where to draw the line
between being professional and getting personal.

———————

6
Do not be afraid to say "I don't know."
Just be sure to follow up that statement with
"I'll find out for you."

Be sure you understand your customer's request.

7

"Can you help me select a shirt?"

If the customer is not specific enough,
ask questions beginning with the words "What. . .,"
"Why. . .," or "How. . ." to gain more information.

"I'd be glad to. What kind of shirt are you looking for?"

(Be careful with your wording
when asking the "Why" question.
It can put your customer on the defensive).

Ask questions beginning with the words
Who. . .," "Where. . .," or "When. . ."
to clarify or discover more specific facts.

*"I can help you find a sport shirt.
Who are you buying it for?"*

———————

How you say it is more important than what you say.

8

———————

If a customer does not understand you,
use different words to explain.
Do not keep repeating the same thing.
It will be frustrating for both of you.

9

10   Use language your customers will understand.
Avoid using company jargon
or technical terms.

———————

11   Never use inappropriate language with a customer.

———————

12   Address the customer by name
if you know it.

———————

13   When you do not know the customer's name,
use sir and ma'am —
but do not overuse these words.
Also, watch how you accentuate them.
Emphasizing "sir" or "ma'am"
can sound condescending.

———————

14   Display empathy.
Let your customer know
you understand how he feels.

15

Words to never use
when a customer asks for another employee:

"_____ is at lunch."

"_____ is on break."

"_____ went home early."

"_____ hasn't come in yet."

"I don't know where _____ is."

16

Words to use
when a customer asks for another employee:

"_____ is unavailable now. May I help you?"

"_____ is out of the office now. May I help you?"

Chapter 6

Listening

L istening is the major component of communication. It is more important than talking. Without the ability to truly listen, communication can never be effective.

1

Listen, listen, listen!

Listen to what
your customers are *really* saying.

2

Listen actively —
Focus entirely on your customer.

3

Remain objective —
Avoid judging.

4

Listen for what is *not* said.

5

Be a complete listener —
Do not be thinking about your response
while the other person is talking.

6

Look directly at the person who is talking to you.

Show interest and empathy
in your facial expressions.

7

———————

Use words like "I see. Tell me more."

8

———————

Do not jump to conclusions.

9

———————

Gather as much information as you can
before making a decision.

10

———————

Do not interrupt the person speaking to you
to answer the phone.

11

═══════════

Chapter 7

Handling Objections

There will be times during your interactions with your customers when they will object to what you are saying, whether it be a sales pitch or a conversation you are having. Never ignore an objection. Sometimes, it may only sound like an objection; in actuality the customer may be looking for more information.

Ignoring an objection will never make it go away. Rather, ignoring it may make the customer go away.

1

Listen to the customer's objection.

"That sounds too expensive."

2

Acknowledge the objection.

*"I can understand
the price may seem a little high. . ."*

3

Respond with a positive statement.
(Respond with a benefit if you are selling something).

*". . .but this product is guaranteed for life,
so when you take that into consideration,
it doesn't seem as expensive
as you might think.
I'm sure you'll be happy with it,
and if you aren't
we will give you a full refund."*

4

Follow up with a question.

"How does that sound?"

5

The customer's response will determine whether he is truly objecting or looking for more information.

"How much did you say it would cost?"
— looking for more information.

"It really sounds too expensive to me."
— objection — time to follow up with a question.

"What were you looking to spend?"
— the customer's response will help you know whether to continue or stop.

If the customer raises another objection, go back to Step 3.

6

Always be truthful
when stating the benefits
or your point of view.
Do not try to glorify the point you are trying to make.
You will come across in a phony manner.

Chapter 8

Giving Your Customer Your Best

C ustomers are self-centered. They come in to your business to see what *you* can do for *them*. They do not care about your or your business. They begin caring for you when they begin trusting you.

1

Go the extra mile for your customer.

2

Find ways to give them more than they expect.

3

Even if there is no competition for your business,
your customers deserve the best service.

4

Treat your customer the same way
you would treat an honored guest invited into your home.

5

Make the customer feel comfortable.

6

After the business transaction, make some follow-up contacts
to insure your customers are satisfied.
Choose customers who may not have been totally pleased,
as well as those who may have additional needs.
This is a great way to make your customers remember you.

7

Appreciate every customer you have.
Tell your customers you appreciate their business.

In multi-cultural situations,
be respectful of the cultural differences.

8

When there is a problem,
try to see things from your customer's perspective.
You'll be surprised how often the customer *is* right.

9

Treat the customer you are helping
as though she were your only customer.
Do not allow yourself to be distracted.

10

When you make a mistake,
make it right with the customer.

11

If there is any doubt in your mind,
always rule in favor of the customer.

12

Never try to prove to a customer she made a mistake.

13

14 After every transaction, ask yourself the following questions:

How well did I handle the customer's request?

How effective and efficient was I?

Was the customer satisfied?

If you cannot answer all the questions positively,
think about what you could have done differently,
and next time, do it.

15

Perception is everything.
To your customer, her perception is *reality.*

16

Treat all customers equally,
no matter their race, religion, or nationality.

17

Send thank you notes
when customers make a large purchase from you.
This will give you another opportunity
to explain the benefits of the product.

18

Always remember . . .

The *customer* is the reason you have a job.

Chapter 9

The Telephone Contact

C onducting business by telephone requires special skills. Because your customer cannot see you, you must verbalize what you are doing. Talking on the phone also requires greater listening ability.

1

Answer on the first ring.

2

When answering the phone, give your company's name,
then your name, then "how may I help you?"
Sound like you really want to help.

3

Listen closely to your customer's opening statement
and respond accordingly.
Never make your customer repeat information
because you failed to listen.

4

Have pen and paper ready and write down
what the customer says, including his name.

5

Let the customer speak without interruption.

6

Establish your credibility.
Let the customer know you can help.

Build rapport with your customer.

7

Address your customer by name,
using Mr., Mrs., or Ms., and the last name.
It is generally all right to use the customer's first name
if the customer has addressed himself by first name;
use good judgment on this and if in doubt ask permission.

8

Your tone is particularly important
since your customer cannot see your body language.

9

Your attitude comes through the phone line — loud and clear.
Make sure yours is a positive one.

10

When you put a customer on hold,
explain why you are doing so.

11

Smile when talking on the phone.
Your customer will "hear" your smile through your voice.

12

13   If you must leave your customer on hold for a lengthy period,
return to the line
to let him know what you are doing
and approximately how long he will be on hold.
Offer to call him back.

---

14   Give your customer your full attention.

---

15   Avoid silence on the line.
Let the customer know what you are doing.

---

16   Vocalize your responses.
Do not assume the person on the other end understands.

---

17   If you are unsure of your customer's request
you will need to ask questions
to gain additional information.
Let your customer know what you will be doing
so he will not wonder why you are "interrogating" him.
Say something like
"I'll need to ask you a few questions in order to help you."

Develop good listening skills.
Sincerely listen to what your customer is saying.
Do not be thinking of your response
while he is talking.

18

Briefly summarize your customer's request
to insure you understand.

19

Before hanging up,
recap what you are going to do for your customer.
Gain the customer's acceptance to make sure
both of you have the same understanding.

20

Before ending the call
give your name again.
Let your customer know you will be
happy to help if he needs to call back.

21

Thank your customer
for calling your business.

22

23

If you need to make a commitment
to call the customer back,
tell him when he can expect to hear from you.

24

Always meet your commitments.

25

When you must call a customer,
either to meet a commitment or to make a sales pitch,
follow the framework below:

Greet the customer.

Introduce yourself and your company.

Be prepared. Know what you are going to say.

Practice delivering your message before you call.

Chapter 10

Face-to-Face Contact

F ace-to-face contact, like telephone contact, requires special skills. Because your customers *can* see your non-verbal body language, it is important to keep actions, gestures and facial expressions positive and non-threatening.

1

Greet your customers
when they walk through your door.

_____

2

Make your customers feel welcome.

_____

3

Smile. Show your enthusiasm for your work.

_____

4

When customers come into your business, remember —
they make your job possible.

_____

5

When a customer leaves your business,
thank her for coming in.
Tell her you hope she comes back soon.

_____

6

Make eye contact when talking to your customer.
It demonstrates trust.

7

Watch your body language and facial expressions.
Keep a positive and friendly demeanor.

8

Help your customer find what she needs.
Do not just point or tell her where she can look.
Show her.

9

Do not be overbearing.
Watch for clues and know which customers
want to be left alone, which customers want your help.

10

Never talk on a personal call
in the presence of customers.

11

When a phone call comes in
while you are helping a customer,
ask the caller to hold while you finish,
or offer to call her back.
Never make the customer
who is there ready to do business
wait while you take a call.

12

Never stand around looking bored.
If you do not have anything to do,
find something to do.

13

Smoking can be offensive to people.
Make it a habit to never smoke
in front of your customers.

Or eat...

Or chew gum...

14

If you make an appointment to meet a customer,
be on time.
Better yet, be early.

=================

Chapter 11

The Difficult Customer

A customer may be difficult to deal with because he is upset, frustrated, or impatient about an interaction with your company, or maybe because he is a gruff person in general. This is the area that requires the most tact to handle. Become familiar with the following tips so you will be confident and comfortable when handling a difficult or irate customer.

1

Never be rude to a rude customer.

2

Be thankful when a customer complains.
He could have just taken his business elsewhere.

3

When a customer complains,
look at it as an opportunity to improve.

4

Put yourself in the customer's shoes.
Try to see the situation from his perspective.

5

Remember,
the customer is not angry at you, personally.
He sees *you* as the company.

6

Do not interrupt
while the customer is telling his story.
Let him get "it" off his chest.

Remain calm. Listen carefully.   7

Focus on the problem, not on the person.   8

When the customer has finished "venting,"
let him know you will do what you can
to rectify the problem.   9

Make sure the customer knows your name.   10

Restate the problem
so your customer knows you understand.   11

Apologize.   12

Display empathy towards the customer's situation.   13

14

Explain what action you will take
to make it right with the customer.

_____

15

Let the customer know
you will take care of the problem
as soon as possible.
Do not make him wait for you to find a convenient time.

_____

16

Offer some sort of compensation,
even if it is a symbolic gesture.
You cannot take away the problem,
but you can do something
to let the customer know you care.

_____

17

Thank the customer
for bringing the problem to your attention.

_____

18

Always, always be sincere.

Follow up with the customer to make sure he is satisfied. 19

Feel proud when you can turn
an upset customer into a satisfied one. 20

If you cannot rectify the problem
to the customer's satisfaction,
let him know you appreciate his point of view. 21

It is all right to ask for the customer's ideas for solutions. 22

When you cannot solve the problem,
tell the customer what you *can* do. 23

Giving good service costs —
only your company knows what price you can afford
to pay to keep a customer.
Sometimes it is not worth your efforts. 24

25

There are times
when you will not win the customer back,
and times when it is not cost effective
for your company to do so.

As an employee, you may have to refer situations
you cannot solve to your manager.
The manager must make the decision
whether your company can afford
the cost of keeping this customer or
whether you need to end the business relationship.

Make sure you and your manager
think this one through thoroughly
before making the final call.

26

Some customers will never be satisfied.
Spend your time and efforts
pleasing those who *can* be satisfied.

Chapter 12

Giving Your Company Your Best

T here is only one person who controls your performance at work. If you think that person is your manager, you are wrong. Your manager does not control how well you are doing. *You* control your performance. *You* are the one who decides how well you perform. You have to be at your job a set number of hours every day. Why not be your best? You will feel good about yourself when you know you have given your all.

1

Give each day 110%.

2

Learn your job well.

3

Have you been trained to do your job?
Do you have the necessary tools to perform?
If not, it is up to you to tell your manager what you need.

4

Ask questions to learn more.

5

Do not expect your manager to be aware of everything.
He has other job duties to perform.
Talk to him about what is going on.

6

If your supervisor does not give you feedback
on your performance, ask for it.

7

Be accountable for your actions.

When you make a mistake,
be up front and tell your boss about it.
Do not wait for her to find out and come to you.

8

Keep up to date on changes in your workplace.
In today's world, change is coming faster and faster.
Learn to be flexible — be ready for change.

9

Being effective and efficient are as important
to your customers as they are to your company.
This means giving customers what they want
quickly and correctly.

10

Being good at what you do makes doing it a pleasure.

11

If you have an idea to improve customer service,
tell your manager about it.

12

Learn from your experiences — good OR bad.

13

14
Never complain about your boss or your company
within earshot of customers.
In fact, never complain about them at all.
If you have a problem, talk to your boss about it.

———————————

15
Think of your place of employment
as if it were your own company.
Think of yourself as the owner when making decisions.

———————————

16
Ask your boss how far you can go to satisfy a customer.
Know your authority limits.

———————————

17
Try to come up with better ways to do a task.

———————————

18
Set performance goals for yourself.

———————————

19
Be innovative.

———————————

20
Be helpful and enthusiastic.

Be enthusiastic about your company, your product, your job. 21

Appreciate the job you have. It will show in your work. 22

Take pride in your business. 23
Keep things clean and neat. (Especially rest rooms).

To the customer, *you* are the company. 24

Be accountable for your company. 25
Use "we" even when referring to another department
or employee in your company.
"I'm sorry, *we* made a mistake" sounds more responsible
than "The *shipping department* messed up."

Be at work on time. There is no excuse for being late. 26

Work until it is time for you to leave. 27
Do not get in the habit of quitting a few minutes early.

28

Measure your own level of performance
by answering the following:

Do you feel good, both physically and mentally?

Are you happy in your job?

Do you look forward to going to work every day?

Do you get along with the other employees and managers?

Are you proud of your efforts?

If you answered yes to the questions,
you are most likely performing well.
If you answered no to any of the questions,
it is time for some self-analysis.

29

Make yourself the best product out there.

30

Have fun in your job!